A World of Difference

Greetings!

By Karin Luisa Badt

CHILDRENS PRESS®
CHICAGO

Picture Acknowledgments

Cover (top left), NASA; cover (top right), © Joe Solem/Tony Stone Images; cover (bottom left), © David Young-Wolff/PhotoEdit; cover (bottom right), © Leonard Lee Rue III/Tony Stone Images; 1, © Richard West/Unicorn Stock Photos; 3 (top right), © Jeff Greenberg/Unicorn Stock Photos; 3 (top left) © SuperStock International, Inc.; 3 (bottom right), © Cameramann International, Ltd.; 4 (left), © Kennon Cooke/Valan; 4 (top), © Rod Furgason/Unicorn Stock Photos; 5 (top left), United Nations; 5 (bottom left), © Keith Wood/Tony Stone Images; 5 (bottom right), © Florent Flipper/Unicorn Stock Images; 6 (left), Charles Gupton/Tony Stone Images; 6 (right), Chip and Rosa de la Cueva Peterson; 7 (top left), The Bettmann Archive; 7 (top right), © Cameramann International, Ltd.; 8 (left), © M. Bruce/Photri; 8 (right), © Robert Frerck/Odyssey/Chicago; 9 (top), © Dennis MacDonald/PhotoEdit; 9 (bottom), © Richard West/Unicorn Stock Photos; 10 (2 photos), © Victor Englebert; 11 (top left), © Jason Laurè; 11 (top right), © Vic Bider/Photri; 11 (bottom), © Kennon Cooke/Valan; 12 (bottom), © Don Smetzer/Tony Stone Images; 12 (top), © Jeff Greenberg/Unicorn Stock Photos; 13 (top), The Bettmann Archive; 13 (bottom left), © Dave G. Houser; 13 (bottom right), © S. Nardulli; 14 (bottom), SuperStock International, Inc.; 14 (top), North Wind Picture Archives; 15 (bottom), Stock Montage; 15 (top), © The Photo Source/SuperStock International, Inc.; 16 (top left and right), © Greg Meadors/ PhotoEdit; 16 (bottom), © Robert Frerck/Odyssey/Chicago; 17 (top), © Martin R. Jones/Unicorn Stock Photos; 17 (bottom), © Photomondo/SuperStock International, Inc.; 18 (bottom), © Kennon Cooke/Valan; 18 (top right), © Eric Sanford/Tom Stack & Associates; 18 (bottom right), © Rich Baker/Unicorn Stock Photos; 19 (bottom), UPI/Bettmann Newsphotos; 19 (top), Chip and Rosa Maria de la Cueva Peterson; 20 (bottom), © Jerry Amster/SuperStock International, Inc.; 20 (top), © Cameramann International, Inc.; 21 (left), © Richard T. Nowitz/Valan; 21 (top right), © Michael Newman/PhotoEdit; 21 (botom right), © Stephen McBrady/PhotoEdit; 22, © Robert Frerck/Odyssey/Frerck/Chicago; 23 (2 photos), © Cameramann International, Inc.; 24 (bottom), © Leonard Lee Rue III/Tony Stone Images; 24 (top), © Tony Freeman/PhotoEdit; 25 (left and top right), UPI/Bettmann Newsphotos; 25 (bottom), © Jason Laure; 26, Stock Montage; 27, © Richard Hutchings/PhotoEdit; 28 (bottom), © Cameramann International, Inc.; 28 (top), © Dave G. Houser; 29, © Jason Laure; 30 (top), Chip and Rosa de la Cueva Peterson; 30 (bottom), © Jason Laure; 31 (left), © Don Smetzer/Tony Stone Images; 31 (right), © Bridgeman Collection/SuperStock International, Inc.

On the cover

Top right: Japanese boys giving
  the peace sign, Hiroshima, Japan
Bottom left: Sisters greeting each
  other with a hug, United States
Bottom right: A holy man using the
  traditional Hindu greeting, India

On the title page

A handshake between friends

Project Editor Shari Joffe
Design Beth Herman Design Associates
Photo Research Feldman & Associates

Badt, Karin Luisa.
   Greetings! / by Karin Luisa Badt.
      p. cm. — (A world of difference)
   Includes bibliographical references and index.
   ISBN 0-516-08188-8
      1. Salutations—Juvenile literature.   [1. Salutations.
   2. Vocabulary.] I. Title. II. Series.
   GT3050.B28 1994
   395—dc20   94-18777
                                                        CIP
                                                         AC

CURR
GT
3050
.B28
1994

Contents

Greetings, Everyone!

Hello! *Bom Dia! Ming-gah-bou! Shalom! Ni-hao-ma!* If you're walking down the street and you see a friend, you probably wave, or smile, or say "Hi." Maybe you do all three! These are all ways of *greeting* your friend. Greetings are things that people say or do to show that they recognize the presence of another person. Every culture in the world uses them.

Romania

Greetings may be quite simple—like smiling or shaking hands—but they are very important. By greeting one another, people confirm that they have some kind of relationship. If they had no relationship, they would just ignore each other!

Greetings are also important because almost every human interaction begins with one. Usually, people do not just start talking to each other; first they greet one another, and then they begin talking.

Canada

Waving Waving is a common greeting in many parts of the world, probably because it is one of the most visible ways to catch someone's attention when you spot them at a distance!

The above phrases mean "hello" in these languages: *Bom dia,* Portuguese; *Ming-gah-bou,* Ga, a language spoken in Ghana; *Shalom,* Hebrew; *Ni-hao-ma,* Chinese

When school begins, your teacher probably says something like "Good morning, class." He or she doesn't just say "Open your math books"!

But does everyone throughout the world greet each other the same way? The answer is no. Every culture has its own rules about how to greet people —what to say and do.

Sudan

Even in the same culture, the rules can differ according to the people and the situation.

People follow their culture's greeting rules without even thinking about it. Do you say "Good morning" to neighbors you see on your way to school? If you do, it's because in your culture, this is the polite way to greet a neighbor in the morning. You probably *wouldn't* say "Yabba-dabba-doo!"

China

Two non-human friends
Greetings are important for other species, too!

Handshake, Bow, or Hug?

Greetings are more than just words. Body language—the way you stand, the look on your face, the movements you make—also plays a large role. And the way people use their bodies when they greet each other varies from culture to culture. Do people bow their heads or shake hands? Do they come close to the other person or stay far away? In some countries, people actually touch the other person, while in others, this would be considered impolite.

Bedouin men stroke their beards when they meet someone. The Polynesians of Tahiti rub noses. Japanese people bow; the more important the person being greeted, the lower the bow.

Friends meeting on the street, Mexico How close people stand to one another when greeting—as well as whether they touch each other or not—varies from culture to culture. In Mexico, it is considered acceptable for male friends to greet each other with an embrace.

Japanese businessmen In Japan, it is the custom to bow when greeting someone. An *eshaku* (a slight bow) is for friends and business associates. A *futusurei* (a medium bow) is for people with whom you are not as close. And a *saikeirei* (a deep bow, almost to the floor) is used when meeting extremely important people. It is not used much.

Maori women, New Zealand
Pressing noses together, a custom called *hongi*, is the traditional way Maori people greet each other.

Aymara women, Bolivia
This woman says hello to a friend with a tip of her bowler hat.

Ecuadorians at a marketplace
This Ecuadorian woman is greeting her friend with *medio abrazo* ("half embrace")—a sort of partial hug.

Moroccan friends

In many countries in Europe, the Middle East, and Latin America, friends kiss each other on the cheeks every time they meet. The number of kisses depends on the country. In Mexico, you give a friend just one kiss on the cheek. In Egypt, people kiss three times: first on one cheek, then on the other, and then back to the first cheek. And if you ever go to Italy, get ready to pucker up. People there kiss each other *four* times—twice on each cheek!

Mexico In Mexico, friends often greet each other with one kiss on the cheek.

Businesspeople, United States
In the United States, businesspeople usually shake hands when meeting each other.

Shaking hands, like kissing, is popular throughout the world. In some places, like Germany, friends usually greet each other with a handshake. In other places, like the United States, handshakes tend to be used mainly when meeting someone for the first time, or in a business situation, such as a job interview.

The handshake has been with us for thousands of years. Originally, men shook hands with each other to show that they were not carrying weapons.

Handshake Clasping the hand of another person is a gesture of greeting that has been around for thousands of years.

Some cultures have greetings that involve a series of actions. The Tuareg are a nomadic people who live in the western Sahara—a huge desert in Africa. In some regions, the Tuareg greet each other by lightly touching each other's hand repeatedly while asking many courteous questions. A Tuareg who reaches the camp of other Tuaregs will stop at a certain distance, 150 feet or more depending on the terrain, and wait patiently to be noticed. At that time, a man (if there is one present, and if not, a woman) will walk to him and greet him. If the greeter is a man, he will, just as the guest, have carefully rewound his *tagilmust* (turban-veil). Often, after that, the two will sit on the ground and exchange news for some time before walking back to the tents. This gives the people in the camp some time to attend to their own appearance. When a guest leaves, someone or several people from the camp will walk with him for a certain distance.

Tuareg greetings Among the Tuareg, greetings often involve a series of actions. These photographs show two stages of a meeting between Tuaregs of different groups: a visiting Tuareg exchanging news with his hosts before being invited back to their camp (left), and Tuareg women escorting a departing visitor from their camp (above).

Eye contact is part of body language, and whether or not you look people in the eye when you greet them may depend on your culture. Indonesians, Chinese, and Japanese think that too much eye contact is a sign of bad manners. Many American Indians feel the same way. The Navajo, for example, think that looking someone straight in the eye means you don't believe what the person is saying.

In other cultures, it is considered rude *not* to look someone in the eye. Arabs, for example, tend to look deeply into each other's eyes. They believe that direct eye contact shows interest in the other person. Koreans also look people in the eye. They believe that the eyes show what a person is really feeling and thinking.

Eye contact In Egypt (top left), Greece (below), and the United States (above), people tend to make a lot of eye contact while greeting someone.

Friend, Family, or Foe?

The way people greet each other shows something about their relationship. In most cultures, people greet family members and friends differently than they greet other people. You wouldn't say "How do you do, sir?" to your best friend. If you did, he would wonder what was wrong with you! "How do you do?" is a formal greeting, used when you want to be very polite and respectful. Similarly, you wouldn't say "Hi, how's it going?" or "Hey, what's up?" to your school principal. Those are the informal or casual kinds of greetings you would use with your friends.

Every culture has its own rules about appropriate greetings. In Turkey, people say *"Merhaba"* ("hello") when they meet their friends. However, when greeting someone for whom they want to show respect, they say *"Nasilsiniz"* ("How are you?"). The Zulu of South Africa greet friends with *"Sakubona."* They say *"Sanibona"* when greeting someone with whom they have a more formal relationship. In Italy, friends and relatives say *"Ciao"* ("hi") to each other. They never say *"Ciao"* to people they don't know very well. Instead, they may say *"Buon giorno"* ("Good day") or *"Buona sera"* ("Good evening").

Friends

Formal vs. informal greetings
Your body language—not just your words—varies according to *who* you are greeting. For example, with friends or family, you might use an informal greeting like a hug. But with a clergy person, you'd probably use a more formal greeting, such as a handshake.

Parishioners and priest

12

So very pleased to meet you . . . In the past, it was common in Europe and the United States for a man to greet a woman he liked or respected by kissing her hand.

Italy In Italy, friends often greet each other by saying *"Ciao!"*

South Africa The Zulu of South Africa say *"Sakubona"* when greeting friends.

Most cultures have rules about how you greet people who are superior to you in some way. "Superiors" may be people who have a higher position in society than you do because of their job, their age—or even, in some cultures, because of their gender!

Throughout the world, members of the armed forces salute their commanding officers. Among the native people of Fiji, men are expected to say "O-o-oooooo" when greeting their chief. In Brazil, you would say *"Vossa Senhoria"* when greeting a judge, and *"Vossa Magestade"* to a king. In Madagascar, people used to greet nobles by saying *"Tsara Va?"*, which means "Are you well?" In the United States, you might say "It's an honor to meet you" to someone in a high position. In many cultures, children greet older people in a special way to show their respect. Hindu children in India may greet their parents by crossing their arms while looking away and keeping silent. In Japan, children

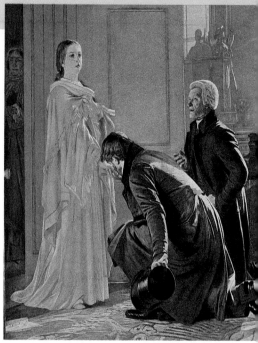

Queen Victoria of England (1819-1901) being greeted by one of her subjects In most cultures, people who have very high status in their society, such as government leaders or royalty, are greeted very formally.

United States military cadet In many countries, members of the armed forces greet their commanding officers with a salute.

are taught to bow slightly when greeting a grown-up. Austrian students may stand up when their teacher enters the classroom. In the Middle East, it's the custom for a child to greet an older person by taking that person's hand, kissing it, and bringing it to his or her own forehead. This custom is most common between children and grandparents, especially if the grandparent has given the child a gift!

In some cultures, whenever two people meet, one of them is always considered more important than the other. This is the case among the Wolof, a Muslim people who live in Senegal and The Gambia. They have a saying, "When two persons greet each other, one has shame, the other has glory."

Prince Andrew greeting the Queen Mother Most people would greet royalty, such as England's Queen Mother, quite formally. Her grandson Prince Andrew, however, gets to greet her with a kiss, because to him, she's family!

Gladiators, ancient Rome Gladiators were men who were forced to fight each other—usually to the death—for the amusement of the public in ancient Rome. When the gladiators entered the arena, they greeted the emperor by saying *"Morituri te salutamus"* —"We who are about to die salute thee!"

What's Going On?

The way people greet each other often depends on the situation. A salesclerk may greet a customer by saying "May I help you?" A person who is giving a speech may begin by saying "Greetings, ladies and gentlemen." A judge may say "Please rise."

In many cultures, people change their greetings depending on the time of day. In English-speaking cultures, people might say "Good morning," "Good afternoon," or "Good evening." In France, people say *"Bon jour"* ("Good day") during the day and *"Bon soir"* ("Good evening") in the evening. The Afrikaners of South Africa say *"Goeie more"* in the morning, *"Goeie middag"* in the afternoon, and *"Goeie naand"* in the evening.

In some cultures, there is a special greeting for almost every situation! This is true for the Yoruba people of Nigeria. A person who goes to the

Little leaguers, Hawaii
In some sports, members of the opposing teams greet each other by shaking hands before the beginning of the game.

Woman receiving diploma
In English-speaking countries, when someone graduates from school, the proper greeting is "Congratulations!"

Vietnamese store in Quebec, Canada A Vietnamese salesperson might greet a customer by saying *Chào ông bà, Tôi có thê giúp ông bà nhữ'ng gì?* "(Hello, may I help you?)."

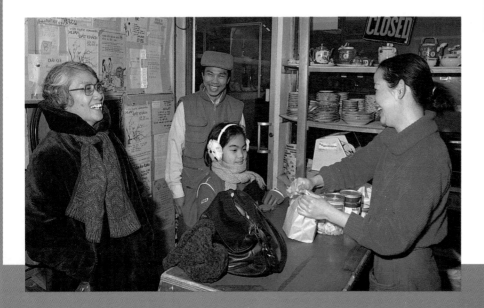

hairdresser greets him or her by saying *"E ku e wa"* ("Greetings for beauty"). People greet a pregnant woman with the words *"A so ka le anfaani"* ("I wish you a safe delivery"). If it hasn't been raining for a while, people say *"E ku ogbele yi"* ("I greet you for this dry season").

How do you pick up the phone? Modern technology has introduced new situations that require greetings: such as answering the telephone. Most people in the United States say "Hello" when they answer the phone. In Cyprus, people answer the phone with *"Ano"* ("Yes"), while people in the Czech Republic say *"Prosim"* ("Ready"). In Germany, people often answer the phone by saying their last name.

French father and son reunited at the end of World War II In certain situations—such as being reunited with someone you love after a long separation— greetings can be quite emotional!

Yoruba society is an example of a culture in which greetings are standardized—in other words, there is one proper thing to say for every occasion, and everyone knows what it is. In some ways, this makes life easier. For example, when someone dies, people don't have to wonder what to say to the family. They use the standard greeting that was invented for that situation, and know that it is the right thing to say.

Japanese businessmen exchanging *meishi* cards
In Japan, when greeting someone in a business situation, it is customary to bow and exchange name cards or business cards, called *meishi* cards.

In other cultures, people invent their own greetings to fit the situation. Some of these greetings are meant to be funny. In China, a person may say *"Xi tou l'a"* to a girl who has come in from the rain. This means "Oh, you've washed your hair!" To greet a friend who has been jogging, a Chinese may say *"Chu han le"* ("You are sweating!") The Chinese use such personal greetings because they feel it is important to make others feel like part of the family, even if they are strangers. Few people in China just say *"Ni-hao-ma,"* which means "How are you?" To them, that sounds too formal.

In almost all cultures, birthdays, holidays, and other times of celebration call for special greetings. In Lebanon, people use the greeting *"Kulla sannah wantum bixer"* ("And every year may you be in good health") for special occasions such as birthdays and New Year's Eve. The Muslims of Senegal

Happy Birthday! In many cultures, times of celebration, such as birthdays, call for special greetings.

celebrate a holiday in honor of Abraham's near-sacrifice of his son Isaac. During this celebration, people greet one another by saying *"Daywaneti,"* which means "Long life to you."

Tet, Vietnam Tet is the Vietnamese New Year festival. It is celebrated for three days beginning on the first new moon after January 20. During Tet, people return to their parents' home, bringing food and gifts. When they arrive, they greet each other with the phrase *"Chúc muñg năm mới."* ("I wish you a happy new year").

Passover *seder,* Israel
During Passover, Jewish people often greet each other by saying *"Chag s'ameach"* ("Happy holiday").

God Jul! Kala Christougenna! Boże Narodzenie! Christmas is a holiday celebrated in many countries. For several weeks in December, many people throughout the world greet each other with their language's version of "Merry Christmas." (The above phrases mean "Merry Christmas" in Swedish, Greek, and Polish).

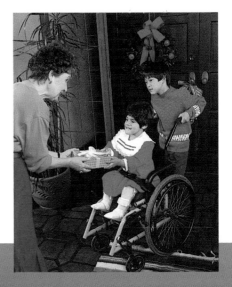

Weddings often involve special greetings. Mayan Indian families of Belize have a feast the evening before a wedding. Before they eat, each person greets everyone else in a specific order. First the groom's father greets the bride's father, and then he greets the bride's mother. Then the groom's mother does the same. Then it is the groom's turn to greet people, and then the bride's. The greeting used by all is *"Ma saala? Ats? Ool?"* It means "Is your heart good?", which is a way of saying "Are you well?" This greeting is ordinarily used only by people who are close to one another. So, this ritual helps establish that everyone is about to become part of a new family. In fact, as part of the ritual, each greeter uses a new title for the other person: father-in-law, mother-in-law, daughter-in-law, son-in-law. For the rest of their lives, these people will greet each other the way they did at the feast. They will always use the intimate greeting "Is your heart good [blank-in-law]?" and shake hands with each other.

Wedding receiving line, Argentina In many cultures, immediately after the wedding ceremony, guests line up to greet the wedding party and offer their congratulations.

Even casual get-togethers involve special greetings in some cultures. In Yemen, men often get together in the afternoons for a "gat chew." They meet at someone's house, where they relax by chewing gat leaves while lying on comfortable cushions and carpets. When a new person arrives, he must decide how to greet the other guests. He looks around to see

Father-in-laws greeting each other at a wedding celebration, India A wedding is a time when two different families are symbolically joined together. So it's not surprising that in many cultures, wedding celebrations involve special greetings.

if there are any important "honored" people. If there are, he must greet them one by one. If there are no such people and the group is small, the newcomer stands by the door and says *"As-salam-tak-kom."* ("Peace be with you"). If the group is large, he says *"Salam tahiyuh"* ("Greetings for peace").

Traditional Korean wedding ceremony During a traditional Korean wedding ceremony, the bride and her assistants greet her future husband with a low bow.

Religious and Political Greetings

Greetings can show something about a person's beliefs. In some religions, people use special greetings with each other. Muslims are followers of the religion known as Islam. When two Muslims meet, one says *"As-salam 'alaykum"* ("Peace be with you"). The other replies *"Wa'alaykum as-salam"* ("Peace be with you too"). In this way, they not only greet one another, but also show that they share the same religious faith.

In India, the traditional greeting among Hindus is called *namaste,* which means "I bow to you." People bow their heads, place the palms of their hands together, and bring their hands to their chests. This greeting expresses the Hindu belief that God exists in everyone. When someone bows to someone else, he or she is recognizing the God in that person. However, many people in India use *namaste* without knowing its original meaning. Bowing has become the common way to greet someone in India, even among those who are not religious.

Greeting during Roman Catholic church service
At a certain point during a traditional Roman Catholic service, the priest says, "Let us offer each other the sign of peace." The members of the congregation then turn to each other, shake hands, and say, "Peace be with you."

Holy man using traditional Hindu greeting, India

President Franklin D. Roosevelt making Victory sign This gesture symbolized a hope for victory during World War II.

Sometimes, members of political groups invent special greetings to use among themselves. By exchanging these greetings, members identify themselves as part of the group and confirm that they share certain beliefs. Members of the Nazi party in Germany always greeted each other with the words *"Heil Hitler"* ("Hail Hitler") to show their support for their leader, Adolf Hitler. When the Nazis took control of Germany in the early 1930s, they required all German citizens to use this greeting on every occasion. Hitler and the Nazis not only started World War II but killed millions of civilians as well. Today, it is illegal to use the Nazi greeting in Germany.

During the years of Communist rule in Czechoslovakia, (1948-90), the proper Communist greeting was *"Čest prāci"* ("There's honor in work").

Peace sign During the turbulent 1960s—when the war in Vietnam and the Civil Rights Movement were the dominant issues in the U.S.— the same gesture became a greeting symbolizing the desire for peace. Here, Shirley Chisholm gives the peace sign in 1968 after becoming the first African-American woman to win a seat in Congress.

Peace sign, South Africa Today, this gesture is a symbol of peace all over the world.

When Greetings are Misunderstood

Cultural differences can lead to misunderstandings when people greet one another. Suppose an American meets an Indonesian. The American looks directly at the Indonesian as they greet. The American is trying to show that she's paying attention. But the Indonesian may be offended by what he thinks is a display of bad manners!

Misunderstanding a greeting can have disastrous results. For example, the Maori of New Zealand

Peaceful meeting between the Maori and European settlers, New Zealand, 1800s
Though cultural differences originally caused some misunderstandings between the Maori and European settlers, they eventually learned to understand each other better.

traditionally greeted strangers by standing up and raising a weapon. When European explorers came to New Zealand in the 1700s, they were greeted this way. However, the Europeans misunderstood. They thought they were about to be attacked, and so they fired their guns at the Maori. Later, as Europeans and Maori had more contact with each other, they learned to understand each other's greetings better.

Today, there are many places where people from different cultures live together. The United States is one such place. The Netherlands is another. People in these countries must learn to be sensitive to one another's ways. For example, a Dutch man of the Netherlands must learn not to feel insulted when the Turkish woman next door refuses to say hello to him. In Turkish culture, men and women who are strangers to one another do not exchange greetings. They must be introduced to one another by someone else first.

Greeting someone in the right way is more important in some cultures than others. For example, in the United States, if you say hello by mistake to someone you don't know, it might not be a big deal. In other parts of the world, greeting someone you don't know could be taken as an insult.

Waving Waving the hand is a common gesture in many countries. However, what it means depends on where you are! In the United States, for example, it usually means "Hello" or "Goodbye." In some Asian countries, it can mean "Please come here." In some parts of Scotland, a hand wave is a terrible insult!

How Do You Respond?

When someone greets you, you don't just stand there—you respond in some way. Just as there are standard greetings, there are standard responses. Sometimes, the response is to repeat the greeting, as when your friend says "Hi" and you say "Hi" back. But when someone says "What's up?" or "What's new?" you don't answer with those same words. If you're like most people, you say "Not much!"—even if a lot *is* going on! Of course, it's understood that "not much" doesn't really mean what it says. There may be a lot that's new. "Not much" is just something to say.

Arab men, Jerusalem Arabs sometimes show their respect by trying to outdo one another in their responses to greetings.

Similarly, most people respond to the greeting "How are you?" by saying "Fine," even if they aren't fine at all. They realize that a greeting like "How are you?" isn't *really* a request for information. It's a way of being polite. It's also a conversation starter.

Traditional greeting, Thailand In some cultures, the proper response to a greeting is to repeat the same word or gesture.

Most conversations don't begin until greetings have been exchanged. Sometimes this takes only a few seconds, but other times, the exchange seems to go on and on! Have you ever heard something like this?

Rosa: "Hi. How are you?"
Andy: "Fine. How are you?"
Rosa: "Fine. So, what's up?"
Andy: "Oh, not much. What about with you?"
Rosa: "Nothing much."

The amount of time people spend greeting each other can differ from culture to culture. In Mali, for example, people ask each other about the health of every member of their families before they start conversing. In various Arab countries, people show respect by trying to outdo one another in their responses to greetings. If one person says *"Marhaba"* ("Hello"), the response may be *"Mit marhaba"* ("A hundred hellos")! If someone says *"As-salam 'alaykum"* ("Peace be with you"), the other person may say *"Wa rahmat allah wa barakatihi"* ("And the mercy of God and his blessing").

Dogon men, Mali In Mali, people ask each other about the health of every member of their families before they start conversing.

Farewells

For every hello, there must be . . . goodbye! A greeting begins an interaction; a farewell ends one. In most cultures, people do not just walk away or hang up the telephone in silence! In Italy, people may end a meeting by saying *"Arrivederci."* The French might say *"Au revoir,"* and Germans and Austrians might say *"Auf wiedersehn."* These are all ways of saying goodbye.

In many languages, saying goodbye means more than "That's all, I'm leaving now." It can also mean "Good luck to you." For example, did you know that the English word "goodbye" comes from the religious expression "God be with you"? And "Farewell" comes from the expression "Fare you well," which is another way of saying "I hope things go well for you."

Saying goodbye can also mean "Don't worry; we'll see each other some other time." *"Arrivederci,"* *"Au revoir,"* and *"Auf Wiedersehen"* all mean "Until we meet again."

Chile

So long, everybody!
Waving can mean hello; it also can mean goodbye!

Nigeria

30

In English, people often say "Talk to you later" or "See you soon." In this way, we reassure one another that our relationships will continue.

That's all, folks! Until next time . . . .

Son leaving for college, United States

Goodbye on the Mersey, by 19th-century French artist James Tissot

Glossary

appropriate proper; suitable (p.12)

confirm to make sure of the truth of (p.4)

courteous polite (p.10)

culture the beliefs and customs of a group of people that are passed from one generation to another (p.4)

custom the usual way of doing things (p.7)

exchange the act of giving and receiving (p.25)

fashionable descriptive of what is popular at a particular time (p.17)

gender a person's maleness or femaleness (p.14)

gesture a motion of the body that expresses an idea or feeling (p.9)

interaction the act of two people relating to one another (p.4)

intimate familiar; marked by close association (p.22)

misunderstanding when something is taken in a wrong sense or way (p.26)

nomadic referring to people who move from place to place (p.10)

reassure to give confidence to; to make sure of again (p.30)

recognize to know and remember upon seeing (p.4)

relationship the connection between two people (p.4)

sacrifice the act or ceremony of making an offering to God or a god (p.21)

standard regularly and widely used (p.20)

status position or rank of a person or thing (p.14)

superior higher in rank or importance (p.14)

symbolic standing for or representing something (p.16)

technology the scientific methods and ideas used in industry and trade (p.19)

traditional handed down from generation to generation (p.7)

turbulent marked by violence or unrest (p.25)

Index

About the Author

Karin Luisa Badt has a Ph.D. in comparative literature from the University of Chicago and a B.A. in literature and society from Brown University. She likes to travel and live in foreign countries. Ms. Badt has taught at the University of Rome and the University of Chicago.